SONGS AND STORIES FROM THE AMERICAN REVOLUTION

Songs and Stories
from the
American Revolution

JERRY SILVERMAN

The Millbrook Press
Brookfield, Connecticut

Photos courtesy of Broadsides Collection, John Hay Library,
Brown University: p. 10;
Library of Congress: pp. 15, 21, 29, 32, 35, 39, 42, 44,
49, 52, 58, 63, 66; Bettmann: pp. 22, 27, 50; North Wind
Picture Archives: p. 56. Map by Joe Le Monnier.

Published by The Millbrook Press
2 Old New Milford Road
Brookfield, Connecticut 06804

Library of Congress Cataloging-in-Publication Data
Songs and stories from the American Revolution / [compiled
by] Jerry Silverman.
1 score
For voice and keyboard instrument with chord symbols.
Contents: The drum—The wars of America—The
sergeant—Yankee Doodle—Ballad of Bunker Hill—The
riflemen of Bennington—The Battle of Saratoga—The
swamp fox—The surrender of Cornwallis—In the days of
Seventy-Six.
Includes bibliographical references (p.   ) and index.
ISBN 1-56294-429-0
1. United States—History—Revolution, 1775–1783—Songs
and music—Juvenile. [1. United
States—History—Revolution, 1775–1783—Songs and
music. 2. Songs.] I. Silverman, Jerry.
M1992.57 1994 94-10658 CIP M

CONTENTS

SONGS AND STORIES FROM THE AMERICAN REVOLUTION

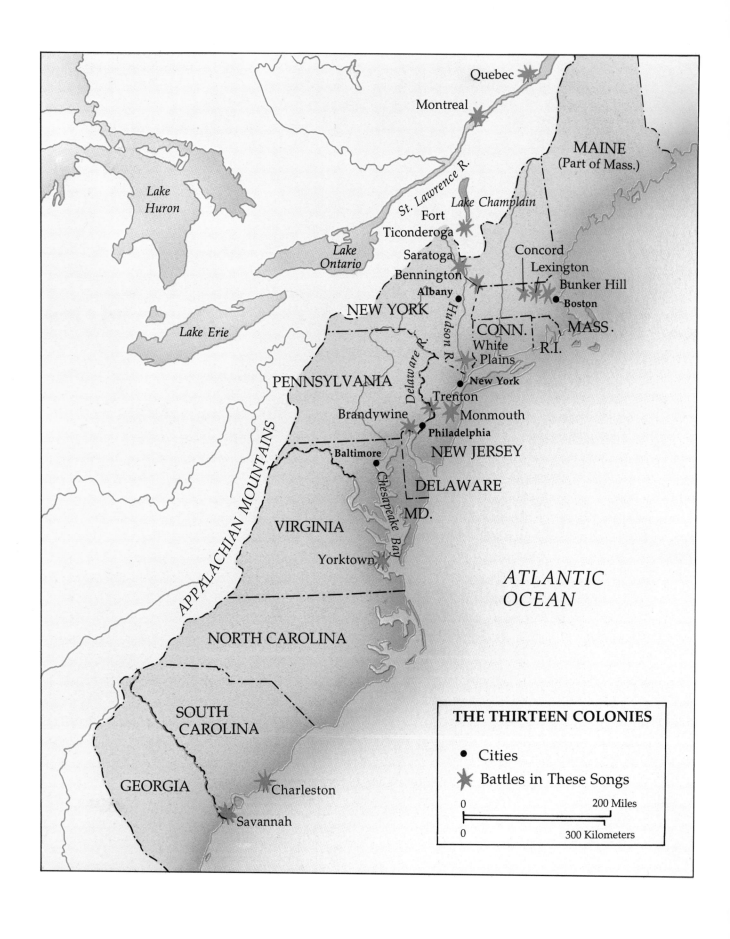

Lake Huron

Lake Ontario

Lake Erie

Quebec

Montreal

St. Lawrence R.

Lake Champlain

MAINE
(Part of Mass.)

Fort
Ticonderoga

Saratoga

Bennington

Concord

Lexington

Bunker Hill

Albany

Boston

Hudson R.

NEW YORK

CONN.

White
Plains

R.I.

MASS.

Delaware R.

New York

PENNSYLVANIA

Trenton

Monmouth

Brandywine

Philadelphia

NEW JERSEY

Baltimore

DELAWARE

Chesapeake Bay

MD.

APPALACHIAN MOUNTAINS

VIRGINIA

Yorktown

ATLANTIC
OCEAN

NORTH CAROLINA

SOUTH
CAROLINA

GEORGIA

Charleston

Savannah

THE THIRTEEN COLONIES

• Cities

✹ Battles in These Songs

0   200 Miles

0   300 Kilometers

INTRODUCTION

This is a collection of songs from the American Revolution and stories about the people who sang them. These songs paint a rich picture of another time and place. When you sing them yourself, the people and dramatic events surrounding the birth of our nation come alive.

In the eighteenth century, many English settlers came to the colonies that Britain owned along the coast of North America. They brought with them a long tradition of ballad singing. Ballads, or stories set to music, were a common form of entertainment in England. A good ballad singer would always draw a crowd, captivating listeners with the strains of music and the drama of a story unfolding.

In the British colonies, while some singers were better than others, professional musicians, as we know them today, did not exist. It was rare for people to have musical instruments in their homes, and musical instruction—if it could be found at all—was a luxury that few could afford. So, except when an occasional fiddler wandered through town, unaccompanied singing was the rule.

In those days—long before radio, television, and recordings—people heard the latest songs by listening to street singers. These wandering performers, who strolled through the English countryside and the streets of cities like London singing to passersby, now began to be heard in Boston, Philadelphia, and New York.

An interested listener could buy penny sheets from the singer, usually just the words of the verses set to well-known tunes. These sheets were called broadsides. People took the broadsides home and, in turn, sang the songs to their families. When a song was a good one, it spread amazingly fast.

Broadsides were written about up-to-date topics. What began to bother people the most was the fact that the laws governing life in the North American colonies were being passed in London, England—some three thousand miles away. What made matters worse, from the colonists' point of view, was that they had no say in the making of those laws. The British government was forever thinking up new ways to raise money by taxing the colonies. In 1764 and 1765, when taxes were placed on sugar and all legal and official documents, the anger of the colonists began to reach the boiling point.

The FARMER and his SON's Return from a Vi...

CAMP:

Together With The

ROSE TREE.

The FARMER and his SON's, &c.

FATHER and I went down to Camp,
    Along with Captain *Goodin*,
And there we fee the Men and Boys,
    As thick as Hafty-pudding ;

CHORUS.

Yankey doodle, keep it up,
    Yankey doodle dandy,
Mind the Mufick and the Step,
    And with the Girls be handy.

And there we fee a Thoufand Men,
    As rich as 'Squire *David*,
And what they wafted every Day,
    I wifh it could be faved.

The 'Laffies they eat every Day,
    Would keep an Houfe a Winter ;
They have as much that I'll be bound
    They eat it when they're a mind to.

And there we fee a fwamping Gun,
    Large as a Log of Maple,
Upon a ducid little Cart,
    A Lead for Father's Cattle.

And every Time they fhoot it off,
    It takes an Horn of Powder,
It makes a noife like Father's Gun,
    On'y a Nation louder.

I went as nigh to one myfelf,
    As 'Siah's Underpinning ;
And Father went as nigh again,
    I tho't the Duce was in him.

Coufin *Simon* grew fo bold
    I tho't he would have cock'd it ;
It fcar'd me fo I fhriek'd it off,
    And hung by Father's Pocket.

And Captain *Davis* had a Gun,
    He kind of clapt his Hand on't,
And ftuck a crooked ftabbing Iron
    Upon the little End on't.

And there I fee a Pumkin-Shell
    As big as Mother's Bafon,
And every Time they touch'd it off
    They fcamper'd like the Nation.

I fee a little Barrel too,
    The Heads were made of Leather,
They knock'd upon with little Clubs,
    And call'd the Folks together.

And there was Captain *Wafhington*,
    And Gentlefolks about him ;
They fay he's grown fo tarnal proud
    He will not ride without them.

He got him on his Meeting-Clothes,
    Upon a Slapping Stallion,
He fet the World along in Rows,
    In Hundreds and in Millions.

The flaming Ribbons in his Hat,
    They look'd fo taring fine ah,
I wanted pockily to get,
    To give to my *Jemimah*.

I fee another Snarl of Men,
    A digging Graves, they told me,
So tarnal long, fo tarnal deep,
    They 'tended they fhould hold me.

It fcar'd me fo I hook'd it off,
    Nor ftopt as I remember,
Nor turn'd about 'till I got Home,
    Lock'd up in Mother's Chamber.

The ROSE TREE.

A Rofe Tree in full bearing,
    Had fweet flowers fair to fee ;
One rofe beyond comparing,
    For beauty attracted me.

Tho' eager then to win it,
    Lovely blooming frefh and gay ;
I find a canker in it,
    And now throw it far away.

How fine this morning early,
    All funfhining, clear and bright !
So late I lov'd you dearly,
    Tho' loft now each fond delight.

The clouds feem big with ...
    Sunny beams no more ...
Farewell ye fleeting hours,
    Your falfhood has chang'd th...

A printed broadside shows one of many versions of "Yankee Doodle."

Songs protesting these taxes began to be sung throughout the colonies, with words such as:

> The cruel lords of Britain, who glory in their shame,
> The project they have hit on they joyfully proclaim;
> 'Tis what they're striving after, our rights to take away,
> And rob us of our charter in North America.

At first these protest songs dealt mainly with money and taxation, but gradually new words and ideas began to creep into them—words such as "freedom" and "liberty." In 1768 colonial poet John Dickinson wrote:

> Come join hand in hand, brave Americans all,
> And rouse your bold hearts at fair Liberty's call;
> No tyrannous acts shall suppress your just claim,
> Or stain with dishonor America's name.
>
> In freedom we're born, and in freedom we'll live,
> Our purses are ready; steady, friends, steady,
> Not as slaves, but as freemen, our money we'll give.

Dickinson's "Liberty Song" was immediately answered by this blast from an unknown poet in England:

> Come shake your dull noddles, ye pumpkins, and bawl,
> And own that you're mad at fair Liberty's call;
> No scandalous conduct can add to your shame,
> Condemned to dishonor, inherit the fame.
>
> In folly you're born, and in folly you'll live,
> To madness still ready, and stupidly steady,
> Not as men but as monkeys the tokens you give.

Things were definitely heating up, and poets and songwriters were right in the thick of it. The following songs give witness to about twenty years of turbulent American history in the 1770s and 1780s, when the Revolutionary War, the war for American independence, was being fought and won. They tell about hope, hardship, and courage. They sing about some of the battles and about the people who fought in them.

And, best of all, they are fun to sing!

The Drum

Wars are often fought for great and noble ideals. The American Revolution was fought for the highest ideal of all: freedom— freedom from British rule for the colonial American people. But no matter how many great leaders make fine speeches filled with wonderful words and inspiring thoughts, it is the common young soldier who does the fighting and the dying.

The common soldier also sings about what is on his mind: the battles, the fear, the bravery, the homesickness. He sings his songs, but he does not usually write them down. It takes a trained musician to do that, and besides, the soldier is generally too busy fighting or marching or training to do much else. We are very lucky when some soldier actually does have the time, ability, and interest to copy down and preserve soldiers' songs for us. Such a man was Captain George Bush of the 11th Pennsylvania Regiment.

George Bush joined the American Army in 1776, when he was twenty-three years old. By 1779 he had risen to the rank of captain. In that year he began to collect the songs that he heard being sung by his comrades. He was the man for the job, because he played the fiddle and was well educated.

Many of the songs that he heard had actually been published already, but soldiers have a way of changing words here and there to bring an older song up-to-date. "The Drum" could very well have been such a song. It has a British-sounding melody, and the words could easily have been sung in London as well as in Boston or Philadelphia. It is a typical, romantic eighteenth-century view of war as a heroic adventure. Its opening line, "Come each gallant lad who for pleasure quits care . . . ," is telling us that war is really a "pleasure." We later learn that army life consists mainly of drinking with your "lass" (girlfriend), and, oh yes, once in a while killing somebody, and then— back to the bottle.

In this song the drum itself becomes the symbol of military life. In verse one the phrase, "to the drum head with spirit repair," means that each soldier should quickly run ("repair") toward the drum, that is, join the army. The "tattoo" is the drumbeat. It sounds like a drumbeat if you repeat it rapidly: "tattoo, tattoo, tattoo. . . ."

In verse two, the "lads" have spent the night merrily drinking until daybreak, when the drum beats reveille (reh-veh-lee), the wake-up call. Of course, they haven't been sleeping at all. But off they go bravely into battle.

After defeating the enemy (in verse three): "Kill'd and wounded how they lie. Helter skelter see them fly," the enemy's drum is heard as it "beats retreat," signaling that the battle has been lost and it is time to move back. Then the victorious soldiers light a victory bonfire—using the French expression "Feu de Joy" (normally pronounced "feh de jwah," but here it would seem to rhyme with "fly.")

Then, in verse four, it's back to the bottle again ("the drum rolls every toast"), as they cheer for America. After the celebration they loosen ("unbrace") the drumhead and pack it away " 'Till a war again calls away."

On September 11, 1777, Captain Bush was gravely wounded at the Battle of Brandywine, not far from Philadelphia. He recovered from his wounds enough to be able to continue soldiering actively until January 1779. By then he was so weakened from his wounds, which had never fully healed, that he had to give up active campaigning. He was transferred to supply and payroll duties, which gave him the opportunity to begin his song collecting. "The Drum" first appeared in print in about 1780.

Captain Bush remained in the army until the end of the war, in 1783. He died in 1797. We owe him a debt of gratitude for being one of the first American collectors of soldiers' songs. He recognized that songs of the soldiers who fought in the American Revolution were worth preserving.

"Spirit of 76," by Archibald M. Willard, 1876.

THE DRUM

2.

Each night gaily, lads, thus we merrily waste,
'Till the drum, 'till the drum, 'till the drum, tells us it is past.
Picket arms at dawn do shine,
And each drum ruffs it down the long line.
Hark the drum beats reveille, hark the drum beats reveille,
    Saluting the day divine.

3.

But hark yonder shot, see the standard alarm.
Hark the drum, hark the drum, hark the drum beats aloud to arms.
Kill'd and wounded how they lie.
Helter skelter see them fly.
Hark their drum beats retreat, hark their drum beats retreat,
    And we'll fire a Feu de Joy.

4.

Now over the bottle, our valour we boast,
While the drum, while the drum, while the drum rolls every toast.
For America now, Huzza!
The work's ne'er done, we'll dance, sing, and play,
And the drum we'll unbrace, and the drum we'll unbrace,
    'Till a war again calls away.

The Wars of America

Although the Revolutionary War was essentially a fight between Great Britain and its American colonies, soldiers from other nations were involved as well. The French, who had a long history of conflicts with the English, came to the support of the Americans. The British army recruited mercenaries from a part of Germany called Hesse. A mercenary is a soldier who joins up to fight in an army (not necessarily from his own country), just for the money. Mercenaries generally do not have a good reputation, and the soldiers from Hesse, called Hessians, were no exception.

Another country that sent its sons to fight alongside the English was Ireland. Ireland had been ruled by England for hundreds of years, and despite many attempts to free itself, it could not stand up to England's superior strength. Since Irishmen were considered by English law to be "subjects of the crown," that is, ruled by English kings, they often had to serve in English armies. They had to fight England's battles although they would much rather have been fighting against England.

One way in which young Irishmen (and Englishmen, too) were persuaded to join the army was by tricking them into it. An army recruiting sergeant would spot a likely young man and offer him a drink. The young man, not suspecting anything, gladly accepted the offer. The sergeant handed him the drink. Unknown to the young man, the sergeant had dropped a shilling—a coin with the king's portrait on it—into the glass. The minute the young man put the glass to his lips, the sergeant, politely but ever so firmly, informed him that he had "taken the king's shilling," and in so doing he had enlisted in the army! If the startled young man objected, a squad of soldiers arrived and marched him away at gunpoint.

England and France had fought each other in America even before the Revolution. France also had colonies in North America. It claimed a vast territory from New Orleans up along the Mississippi River, calling the area Louisiana, in honor of King Louis XIV. But it was in Canada where the French and British empires bumped violently into each other. The war they fought over control of Canada, from 1754 to 1763, was called the Seven Years' War by the French and the French and Indian War by the English and the Americans. The word "Indian" is in the name because the Indian nations living in the region got involved in the war—on the French side. The Indians could not have realized that they stood to lose no matter who won the war.

A good song, a song that tells how real people actually feel, lasts a long time. "The Wars of America" was first sung during the French and Indian War, but since the same cast of characters was involved some twenty years later in the American Revolution, a new generation picked it up and sang it.

The song presents an Irish mother or father's view of war in a far-off land, America. It does not express the heroic sentiments of "The Drum," where war is pictured as a kind of good-time party. Here, three young Irishmen ("two sons and a son-in-law") are sent over the sea to fight in a war that really does not concern them. In "The Drum" only the unnamed enemy gets killed; in "The Wars of America" the worried parent can only say, "But I don't know if I'll see them more."

In verse two, however, some ships appear, and there is hope that "Terry, my own child" will be on board.

In verse three, the singer identifies herself as Terry's mother. She remembers him as he was before he sailed off to war—strong and handsome and in one piece ("To every leg he has one shin.").

In verse four, her worst fears are realized: Terry's young, strong legs have been shot off "at the Yankee's ball." The use of the word ball here has a clever double meaning: A ball is a gala dance party as well as a cannon ball. The sad reality of the "Yankee's ball" contrasts sharply with the happy affair described in "The Drum."

The English use of Irish soldiers continued on into the nineteenth and twentieth centuries. Wounded Irish soldiers returning from yet another far-off battlefield, this time in India, heard a song, "Johnny, I Hardly Knew You," which contained this verse about yet another pair of missing legs:

Where are your legs that used to run, huroo, huroo?
Where are your legs that used to run, huroo, huroo?
Where are your legs that used to run,
When you first went to carry a gun?
I fear your dancing days are done,
Och, Johnny, I hardly knew you.

THE WARS OF AMERICA

1. I have two sons and a son - in - law, Fight - in' in the wars of A -
mer - i - ca. I have two sons and a son - in - law, Fight - in' in the wars of A - mer - i - ca. But
I don't know if I'll see __ them more, Or wheth - er they'll vis - it old Ire - land's __ shore.

Chorus

To my rum - dee - ah, fa - da - did - dle - ah, Whack to the la - dy to my rum - dee - ah.

2.
I spied two ships a-comin' on the sea,
Hulliloo, bubiloo! and I think 'tis he. } (2)
O ships, O ships, will you wait for a while,
Till I find Terry, my own child? *Chorus*

3.
My son, Terry, is neat and trim,
To every leg he has one shin. } (2)
He's mama's pet and darlin' boy,
He's the ladies toy and the girls' own joy. *Chorus*

4.
O wasn't you cunnin', wasn't you cute,
You didn't get away from the Yankee's shoot. } (2)
'Tis not a devilish shin or leg you have at all,
They was all shot away at the Yankee's ball. *Chorus*

A son heads off to join the Revolution, filling those who are
old enough to know the meaning of war with fear and sorrow.

The Marquis de Lafayette leads a cavalry charge at Monmouth, New Jersey, in 1778.
Without help from the French, the American patriots would never have been able to drive off the British.

The Sergeant

Unlike Terry, the unfortunate Irish soldier described in "The Wars of America," François (Franswah), the French soldier in "The Sergeant," did not have to be tricked into joining the army. The French and the English had fought each other for centuries in Europe and on the high seas. When the center of activity moved to North America, they continued their hostilities in the New World. When the American Revolution broke out on April 19, 1775, only twelve years had gone by since the French and Indian War, in which France lost control of Canada to England. The French felt that by aiding the Americans they could strike a blow against their old English enemy.

A French nobleman, the Marquis de Lafayette sailed off to America to help the Americans in their struggle. However, it was not only the French nobility that sided with the Americans. The French Canadians, who had suffered defeat at the hands of the British, felt that war was just too close to them to sit idly by. They were itching to get into the action, too.

The center of military activity nearest to Québec, the province of Canada that had the largest French population, was Boston. It was to Boston that Sergeant François decided to go.

In verse one, François seems to be having a hard time with his father ("My papa, if you do beat me, I will join the army."). Family problems often send young men off into military service. So, François goes across the border and makes his way down to Boston. When he reaches Boston, he is interested in finding out what is going on. He asks, "How many men fired away?" The original version of "The Sergeant" is in French, but that line is in English. François knows how to make himself understood to the Americans.

He is immediately accepted (verse two) and put into the "van" (an abbreviation for "vanguard," the front-line troops).

François doesn't fare much better than Terry did. In verse three, we learn that he has been shot in the jaw, but despite his wounds he is still able to cry out (in English!), "How many men fired away?," while encouraging his men to continue the battle.

By verse four, François is back with his father in Canada. The old man does not show much sympathy for his wounded son. All he says to him is "I told you so," and "you're lucky you're not dead."

THE SERGEANT

1. "My pa - pa, if you do beat me, I will join the ar - my. I'm

off to Bos - ton town, to fight the Eng - lish crown!" At Bos - ton

he was heard to say: "How man - y men fi - red a - way? May I sign

up to - day to earn a ser - geant's pay?" 2. "Oh, ___ can!"

2.
"Oh yes, we'll let you join the fight,
If you do what is right.
We'll put you in the van,
To fight the best you can."
So with a sharp saber so grand,
And with a pistol in his hand,
François did what he could—
Just as a sergeant should.

3.
And so he marched away to war.
The first shot broke his jaw.
François fell to the ground.
They cried "hooray" all 'round.
But then he rose from where he lay,
"How many men fired away?
Don't slow the charge a bit,
Although your sergeant's hit."

4.
"Oh my dear and my good papa,"
Lamented poor François,
"I'm wounded, did you hear,
By a British grenadier?"
"It has turned out just like I said,
Think yourself lucky you're not dead.
Just bear it like a man,
And do the best you can."

The British grenadier who wounded François is a well-known figure in British military history. Grenadiers first came onto the military scene one hundred years earlier with a newly invented weapon, the hand grenade. These grenadiers became known for their heroism, and a song was written about them that was familiar to every Englishman and American: ''The British Grenadiers.'' Here is one verse from that famous song:

Whene'er we are commanded to storm the palisades,*
Our leaders march with fuses and we with hand grenades.
We throw them from the glacis** about the enemy's ears.
Sing tow, row, row, row, row, row, the British Grenadiers.

*wooden walls of a fort
**a raised earthen wall in front of a fort

Yankee Doodle

Listen, my children, and you shall hear
Of the midnight ride of Paul Revere,
On the eighteenth of April, in Seventy-five;
Hardly a man is now alive
Who remembers that famous day and year . . .

So begins the poem "Paul Revere's Ride," by Henry Wadsworth Longfellow, a description of the opening of the Revolutionary War. After more than ten years of increasing tension between Britain and its colonies, the battle over American independence was on.

The fighting began in Massachusetts. Many protests had begun there over taxation and representation, and finally the British moved in their Loyalist troops. On the night of April 18, 1775, British general Thomas Gage marched his troops out of Boston, headed for Concord some twenty miles away. They were to seize and destroy military supplies that the colonists had stored there. Gage's men were seen leaving Boston, and immediately American patriot Paul Revere galloped out ahead of them to warn the people in the countryside, "The British are coming!"

General Gage succeeded in reaching Concord and destroying the supplies, but on the way back to Boston he was attacked in Lexington by a force of Minutemen—Americans ready to fight at a moment's notice. Under heavy fire from behind fences and barns, British troops struggled back to the safety of Boston. But this was just the beginning. Author Ralph Waldo Emerson would later call the first patriot shot fired "the shot heard round the world."

The surest way to popularize an idea in song is to set new words to a familiar melody. As early as 1767, there was mention in Philadelphia of a comic song called "Yankee Doodle."

When the word "yankee" first appeared in print, people were not quite sure what it meant. To this day there is some confusion about its origin. Some people believe it comes from an Indian word; others think it is based on a French word. The strongest possibility is that it

A painting of Paul Revere's dashing midnight ride. It is his cry, "The British are coming!" that has gone down in history as the opening of the Revolutionary War.

comes from the Dutch name for the English colonists: "Jan Kaas," or "Jan Kees." Jan (yan) is Dutch for John; kees means cheese. "John Cheese" was not meant as a compliment. Neither was "Doodle," which means a fool.

"Yankee Doodle" first appeared in print in a London broadside in 1775. Its subtitle was "The Lexington March." The British band played it on the march to Lexington. In those days, European armies played loud music on the way into battle. It cheered up the soldiers and gave them courage. In this case, the strains of the music let the Minutemen know exactly where the British were.

The Minutemen also realized that the British were trying to make fun of them by calling them "Yankee Doodles." In the true spirit of the times, the familiar melody was taken up by the Americans (with new words by a Harvard College student, Edward Bangs) and sung right back at them. It is this version of "Yankee Doodle" that has gone down in American history.

Bangs was a Minuteman who is said to have taken part in the actual fighting on April 19, 1775. We don't know exactly when he wrote the song, but at least one verse (verse eight) could not have been written before July 3, 1775. That was the day George Washington took command of the American army in Boston.

In verse one, a boy visits a rebel, or patriot, camp with his father. The entire song is a light-hearted description of his impressions of the soldiers, captains, and arms. "Hasty pudding" was a quickly prepared cornmeal mush.

> Yankee Doodle went to town
> Riding on a pony;
> Stuck a feather in his cap
> And called it macaroni.

This well-known verse doesn't seem to have anything to do with the rest of the song. Most people who sing it probably assume that it is just a bit of Revolutionary War nonsense. Not at all!

This verse was sung by the British to taunt the patriots. In eighteenth-century England, a "macaroni" was a gentleman who wore overly fancy clothes in what he thought was the "Italian style," to try to make himself look more important than he really was. In other words, a macaroni was a dandy.

And just what was Yankee Doodle trying to do? He was, from the British point of view, getting "all dressed up" and "putting on airs." Yankee Doodle, in this verse, represents the colonies and their foolish desire to be free of Great Britain.

An engraving of a minuteman, entitled simply "76." These volunteer
soldiers were the first to take on the British army and to sing
their own mocking version of the British song "Yankee Doodle."

In verse three, " 'lasses" means molasses. A "swamping gun"
(verse four) was a large cannon. "Tarnal proud," in verse eight, means
extremely proud. In verse nine, "He set the world along in rows"
means that Washington lined up his troops. "Taring" (verse ten) was
the word for "very," and "pockily" meant "very much." As to who
Jemimah was, it's anybody's guess.

YANKEE DOODLE

2.
And there we see a thousand men
As rich as Squire David,
And what they wasted every day,
I wish it could be saved. *Chorus*

3.
The 'lasses they eat every day
Would keep a house a winter;
They have as much that I'll be bound
They eat it when they're a mind to. *Chorus*

4.
And there we see a swamping gun,
Large as a log of maple,
Upon a deuced little cart,
A load for father's cattle. *Chorus*

5.
And every time they shoot it off,
It takes a horn of powder,
It makes a noise like father's gun,
Only a nation louder. *Chorus*

6.
And Captain Davis had a gun,
He kind of clapped his hand on't,
And stuck a crooked stabbing iron
Upon the little end on't. *Chorus*

7.
I see a little barrel, too,
The heads were made of leather,
They knocked upon with little clubs,
And called the folks together. *Chorus*

8.
And there was Captain Washington,
And gentle folks about him;
They say he's grown so tarnal proud
He will not ride without them. *Chorus*

9.
He got him on his meeting-clothes,
Upon a slapping stallion,
He set the world along in rows,
In hundreds and in millions. *Chorus*

10.
The flaming ribbons in his hat,
They looked so taring fine, ah,
I wanted pockily to get
To give to my Jemimah. *Chorus*

British troops are coming ashore from a man-of-war, which is firing on
a nearby town during the Battle of Bunker Hill.

Ballad of Bunker Hill

When the King of England started pushing Yankees around,
They had a little trouble up in Boston town.
There was a brave Negro, Crispus Attucks was the man,
Was the first one to fall when the fighting began.

The "little trouble" described in this modern song took place on March 5, 1770. Loyalist troops, who had been brought in to enforce British laws of taxation, fired on a group of rebellious colonists. Ex-slave Crispus Attucks was the first of five Americans to be killed in what came to be known as the Boston Massacre.

Five years later, there was more than "a little trouble up in Boston town." And this time, many more than five men were to lose their lives.

On the evening of June 16, 1775, about eight hundred troops from Massachusetts and two hundred from Connecticut, under the command of Colonel William Prescott, were sent out to fortify and occupy two high hills, Bunker and Breed's, near the north shore of Boston. They worked through the night to build a dirt fort on top of Breed's Hill (which is now commonly called Bunker Hill). At daybreak they were discovered by the British, who began to fire at them from their men-of-war (navy ships) in Boston Harbor and from nearby cannons.

British general Gage sent a force of more than 2,300 troops, under the command of Major General William Howe, with orders to attack the Americans and drive them from the hill.

The patriots were outnumbered by more than two to one. They were in a tight spot, and they knew it. There was no way that, behind the dirt wall of their fort, they could be supplied with ammunition once the battle had begun. They could not waste their precious gunpowder and bullets by shooting wildly at the advancing British troops.

The Americans were ordered: "Don't one of you fire until you see the whites of their eyes!"

Closer and closer came the British, advancing slowly and steadily up the hill. The Americans held their fire. The British were peppering the defenders with shot and shell. When the first wave of British redcoats was practically at the fort, the order was given: FIRE!

With a roar, the American guns opened up. Down went the leading ranks of redcoats. Caught by surprise, they quickly retreated down the hill, only to regroup and attack once more. Once more they were driven back.

A third time the line of redcoats marched up the hill. The patriots, many of whom were now out of ammunition, were forced to give up their positions and run for their lives. The British had won the day.

Or had they? British losses were very heavy. One thousand and fifty-four men were either killed or wounded. The Americans suffered a loss of four hundred and fifty men—captured, killed, or wounded.

Both sides had paid a high price. But the British, in capturing the hill, had lost almost half their men. They were so stunned by their losses and by the fierce fighting of the young American army that they never took full advantage of their victory. They failed to fortify the area, and by March 1776, George Washington, who was by then in command of the American army, drove the British out of Boston.

In verse one of "Ballad of Bunker Hill," "The soldiers" are the British. "Columbia" (verse two) is a poetic name for America.

Crispus Attucks was a slave who ran away from his owner in Framingham, Massachusetts, on September 30, 1750. He was twenty-seven years old at the time, and for the next twenty years he lived a free life as a sailor. After many voyages, he felt he should return to America to join the patriot cause. That was why, on March 5, 1770, he found himself at the head of the group that had gathered to speak out against British taxation. And that was how it came to be that, when the British soldiers opened fire, ex-slave Crispus Attucks was the first American killed in what was soon to become the American Revolution.

The bloodiest battle of the war was fought on Bunker Hill.

BALLAD OF BUNKER HILL

2.

Let the foeman draw nigh till the white of his eye
Comes in range with your rifles, and then let it fly,
And show to Columbia, to Britain and fame,
How justice smiles awful when freemen take aim!

3.

But when they got ready and all came along,
The way they marched up the hillside wasn't slow;
We were not a-feared and we welcomed 'em strong,
Held fire till the word and then laid the lads low.

4.

But who shall declare the end of the affair,
At sundown there wasn't a man of us there;
We didn't depart till we'd given 'em some,
We used up our powder and had to go home!

The Riflemen of Bennington

In June 1777, British general John Burgoyne marched his troops down from Canada, heading for Albany, New York. He hoped to link up with troops under the command of General Howe, who would be advancing northward along the Hudson River from New York City. The idea was to control the Hudson Valley, thereby cutting New England off from the rest of the colonies and increasing Great Britain's chances of winning the war.

The problem with these long-distance battle plans was that there was no way for Burgoyne at the northern end to communicate rapidly with Howe at the southern end. On July 30, Burgoyne reached Fort Edward on the Hudson, about 45 miles (72 kilometers) north of Albany. But he was having a difficult time making his way through the deep woods. Meanwhile, instead of moving up the Hudson, Howe set off to attack Philadelphia, the patriot capital.

At Fort Edward, Burgoyne was in a desperate situation. His men were running low on food and ammunition. Their supplies came from Montreal, Canada, which was a long way off. He had hoped that the local population would come to his aid, but Americans remained true to the patriot cause. Then he talked local Indians into fighting for the British against civilians, and angered people even more.

Burgoyne needed to do something quickly to take the pressure off his troops. On August 13, he sent a force of twelve hundred men to Bennington—about 35 miles (56 kilometers) to the southeast—to capture supplies and terrorize the countryside. The commanding officer was the Hessian colonel Friedrich Baum.

Baum was met by nearly two thousand Green Mountain Boys, militiamen from part of New Hampshire (now Vermont) and Massachusetts under General John Stark. "Johnny" Stark's Green Mountain Boys soundly defeated the enemy, killing three hundred men and capturing more than seven hundred. Baum himself died from his wounds. This American victory put an end to the British plan to control the Hudson Valley and cut off New England. It was a turning point in the war.

Although this battle is called the "Battle of Bennington," it was actually fought about 5 miles (8 kilometers) away, near the town of Hoosick, New York. The Bennington Battle Monument, a 301-foot (92-meter) shaft, was once the tallest battle monument in the world.

"The Riflemen of Bennington" baits the British by flaunting the superior courage of the Green Mountain Boys. The lyrics are from a version sung by John Allison. In verse three, "briny water" means the salty water of the Atlantic Ocean. "Bullocks" are young bulls.

Ethan Allen, who organized the Green Mountain Boys, shows them a plan of attack. These soldiers fought bravely for independence from Britain and also to make Vermont, then part of New Hampshire, an independent state.

THE RIFLEMEN OF BENNINGTON

In our hands will prove no tri - fle._____ For the tri - fle._____

2.
Ye ride a goodly steed,
Ye may know another master,
Ye forward come with speed,
But ye'll learn to back much faster.
When ye meet our mountain boys
And their leader, Johnny Stark,
Lads who make but little noise,
Lads who always hit the mark! *Chorus*

3.
Had ye no graves at home
Across the briny water,
That hither ye must come
Like bullocks to the slaughter?
If we the work must do,
Why the sooner 'tis begun,
If flint and trigger hold but true,
The quicker 'twill be done. *Chorus*

General Benedict Arnold was seriously wounded during the
Battle of Saratoga. He later became a traitor to the patriot cause.

The Battle of Saratoga

> When Jack, the King's commander bold,
> Was going to do his duty,
> Through all the crowd he smiled and bowed,
> To every blooming beauty.
> The city rung with feats he'd done
> In Portugal and Flanders,
> And all the town thought he'd be crowned
> The First of Alexanders.

Despite the promise of glory expressed in this unknown poet's verse, General John "Jack" Burgoyne never got the chance to become another Alexander. During the fourth century B.C., Alexander the Great conquered and built a huge empire that extended all the way from Macedonia, on the Adriatic Sea, to Egypt and India. Burgoyne's career began with promise but ended on the banks of the Hudson, near Saratoga, New York, on October 17, 1777.

From the start, Burgoyne's plan to lead his men down from Canada, where he would join General Howe to take control of the Hudson Valley, met with difficulty. The lack of cooperation between Burgoyne's army in the north and Howe's army in the south meant that Burgoyne and his troops would have to take over the entire region on their own.

British troops were first overwhelmed by the Green Mountain Boys outside of Bennington in the summer of 1777. In the fall the Battle of Saratoga raged. There were actually two battles of Saratoga, one on September 19 and another on October 7.

Burgoyne had pushed down by way of Lake Champlain and Lake George and approached the American army under General Horatio Gates. Gates's troops were holed up in a fortified camp near Stillwater on the west bank of the Hudson about 24 miles (39 kilometers) north of Albany.

On September 19, Burgoyne attacked the left side of the American defenses, which were commanded by General Benedict Arnold. Both sides fought fiercely in densely wooded country. By nightfall neither side could claim victory, but the British army had suffered heavy losses, especially among its officers. The two opposing armies withdrew and awaited the next engagement.

General Burgoyne surrenders to General Gates. This patriot victory
at Saratoga was a turning point in the war.

On October 7, the British attacked again. The Americans drove
them back and kept up the pressure by following closely on the heels
of the retreating British troops. On the 16th, Burgoyne and his men
were nearly surrounded. On the 17th he surrendered, with about six
thousand men, near the present-day village of Saratoga Springs.

This tremendous American victory was celebrated by many ballads
and broadsides. The unknown poet who wrote "The Battle of
Saratoga" set his verses to the tune of the Irish song "Brennan on the
Moor."

The original version of "The Battle of Saratoga" is at least twenty-one verses long. It recounts every aspect of the battle in the greatest detail, leaving very little to the imagination. This was the typical style of an eighteenth-century narrative (storytelling) ballad. This somewhat shortened version still gives a good picture. General Burgoyne sails down Lake Champlain from Canada into New York, arriving at Ticonderoga, where he begins his overland march. He attacks. The Americans retreat. The Americans counterattack. Brave men fight on both sides. The British are forced to flee, "burning all their luggage." Burgoyne surrenders.

In verse two, "Tory crew" refers to the Tories, who were royalists, or supporters of British rule. "Ticonderoga" (verse three) refers to Fort Ticonderoga on the northern tip of Lake George. It was captured by the British on July 5, 1777, and abandoned after Burgoyne's surrender.

"St. Clair," in verse four, refers to Major General Arthur St. Clair, who ordered the withdrawal of American troops from Fort Ticonderoga. "Mount Defiance" was a fortified British position just south of Fort Ticonderoga.

The only natural substance hard enough to cut a diamond is another diamond. " 'Tis diamond now cut diamond," in verse nine, is a way of saying that the two opposing armies were of equal strength.

The last verse is also typical of the narrative ballad style. The singer tells us that "my song is at an end," and leaves us with a noble thought, "And vain is their endeavor who strive to do us harm"—anybody who might try to harm us would have no chance to succeed.

Here is a Vermont view of the battle:

In seventeen hundred and seventy-seven,
General Burgoyne set out for Heaven;
But as the Yankees would rebel,
He missed his route and went to Hell.

THE BATTLE OF SARATOGA

1. Come un - to me, ye he - roes, whose hearts are true and bold,____ Who

val - ue more your hon - or than oth - ers do your gold;____ Give ear un - to my

sto - ry and I the truth will tell,____ Con - cern - ing man - y a sol - dier who

for his coun - try fell.____ Who for his coun - try fell,____ who for his coun - try

fell,_____ Con - cern - ing man - y a sol - dier who for his coun - try fell._____

2.

Burgoyne, the king's commander, from Canada set sail,
With full eight thousand reg'lars, he thought he could not fail;
With Indians and Canadians and his curséd Tory crew,
On board his fleet of shipping, he up the Champlain flew.
    He up the Champlain flew, he up the Champlain flew,
    On board his fleet of shipping, he up the Champlain flew. } *Chorus*

(Each chorus is constructed similarly out of the last line of its verse.)

3.

Before Ticonderoga, the first day of July,
Appeared his ships and army, and we did them espy.
Their motions we observed full well both night and day,
And our brave boys prepared to have a bloody fray. *Chorus*

4.

Our garrison they viewed them, and straight their troops did land,
And when St. Clair, our chieftain, the fact did understand,
That they the Mount Defiance were bent to fortify,
He found we must surrender or else prepare to die. *Chorus*

5.

The fifth day of July, then, he ordered a retreat,
And when next morn we started, Burgoyne thought we were beat.
And closely he pursued us, till when near Hubbardton
Our rear guards were defeated, he thought the country won. *Chorus*

6.

And when 'twas told in Congress that we our forts and left,
To Albany retreated, of all the north bereft;
Brave General Gates they sent us, our fortunes to retrieve,
And him with shouts of gladness, the army did receive. *Chorus*

7.

The nineteenth of September, the morning cool and clear,
Brave Gates rode through our army, each soldier's heart to cheer;
"Burgoyne," he cried, "advances, but we will never fly;
No, rather than surrender, we'll fight him till we die." *Chorus*

8.

The news was quickly brought us the enemy was near,
And all along our lines then there was no sign of fear;
It was above Stillwater we met at noon that day,
And everyone expected to see a bloody fray. *Chorus*

9.

Six hours the battle lasted, each heart was true as gold,
The British fought like lions, and we like Yankees bold;
The leaves with blood were crimson, and then brave Gates did cry—
"'Tis diamond now cut diamond! We'll beat them, boys, or die." *Chorus*

10.

The seventh day of October, the British tried again,
Shells from their cannon throwing, which fell on us like rain;
To drive us from our stations, that they might thus retreat;
For now Burgoyne saw plainly, he never could us beat. *Chorus*

11.

But vain was his endeavor our men to terrify;
Though death was all around us, not one of us would fly.
But when an hour we'd fought them and they began to yield,
Along our lines the cry ran, "The next blow wins the field!" *Chorus*

12.

Then burning all their luggage, they fled with haste and fear,
Burgoyne with all his forces, to Saratoga did steer;
And Gates, our brave commander, soon after him did hie,
Resolving he would take them or in the effort die. *Chorus*

13.

As we came nigh the village, we overtook the foe,
They'd burned each house to ashes, like all where'er they go.
The seventeenth of October, they did capitulate,
Burgoyne and his proud army did we our pris'ners make. *Chorus*

14.

Now finished is my story, my song is at an end;
The freedom we're enjoying we're ready to defend;
For while our cause is righteous, heaven nerves the soldier's arm,
And vain is their endeavor who strive to do us harm. *Chorus*

Horatio Gates holds the "Article of Capitulation" announcing Burgoyne's defeat. Americans were so thrilled by this brilliant victory that many thought Gates should replace Washington as commander of all the patriot troops.

General Francis Marion became known as "The Swamp Fox" for his cunning escape from the British into the swamps near Charleston, South Carolina.

The Swamp Fox

On July 27, 1689, some eighty-six years before the American Revolution, the British found themselves engaged in another battle against a people fighting for their freedom. It was in Killiecranckie, Scotland, and the Scots were victorious that day. But their heroic leader, John Graham, Viscount (vy-count) Dundee, was killed in the fight. His supporters called him Bonnie (handsome) Dundee, and they sang a song about him with a galloping melody and words like: "Come fill up my cup and fill up my can, Come saddle my horses and call out my men. . . . For it's up with the bonnets of Bonnie Dundee."

When a song was written about Francis Marion (1732–1795), an American officer who led the British on many a merry chase through the swamps of South Carolina, the melody chosen to express his galloping through the wilderness was "Bonnie Dundee."

Francis Marion was born in South Carolina the same year that George Washington was born in Virginia. He knew his way around the backwoods and the swamps, having fought the Cherokees in 1759. By 1775 he had become a captain in the South Carolina militia. Over the next few years he took part in the fighting in South Carolina and Georgia. When Charleston, South Carolina, was captured by the British on May 12, 1780, Marion slipped away into the swamps with a small force of men.

He was able to attack the British by surprise, even though his troop consisted of about seventy men at most. The British, with their large, organized army, could never figure out where Marion was going to strike next, and they could never follow him and catch him in the murky swamps.

The British colonel, Banastre Tarleton, who had repeatedly tried, and failed, to hunt Marion down, paid him a soldier's compliment: "As for this damned old fox, even the devil himself could not catch him."

From then on, Francis Marion was known to friend and foe alike as "The Swamp Fox."

Marion continued his guerrilla warfare against the British, with many daring and successful attacks until the war's end. By that time he had risen to the rank of brigadier general. After the war he was

Many stories were told about Marion's ragtag group of men, whose
surprise attacks caught the British off guard time and again.

elected to the State Senate. In a time when opposing armies usually
either took up fixed positions, or charged openly at each other, "The
Swamp Fox" was truly an original!

The song "The Swamp Fox" is unusual for its time in history. Rather
than going into specific details about this battle or that attack, it creates
a mood, an *impression* of mysterious movement through the swamps.
It is full of images of nature contrasted with the life of the men in the
swamps. It mentions Tarleton only once, describing how "we burrow

in the cypress tree'' to escape from him. The ''turfy tussock'' (verse one) is a thick clump of grass, an ideal hiding place.

In the eighteenth century, military battles were almost always fought in the daytime. There was no way opposing armies could see each other at night. In verse two, we see that Marion's men ''shun'' (avoid) the light of day, preferring to attack on ''chargers'' (horses) at night while the enemy is sleeping: ''And ere (before) he drives away his sleep . . . he dies.''

In verse three, the ''gallant steed'' (brave horse) and rider swim across the Santee River to escape the pursuing enemy, while fighting back with ''twisted bore'' (referring to the barrel of a gun) and ''smiting brand'' (striking sword).

In verse four, the men are cooking and eating—ordinary but necessary occupations. (Contrast this with life as pictured in ''The Drum,'' where the only nourishment ever taken seems to come out of a bottle.)

In verse six, we get an interesting picture of ''the colonel'' (Marion) that describes him at his evening prayers.

The ''hoecake'' in verse seven is cake made out of cornmeal, so called because it was often baked on the blade of a hoe. A typical Southern food, it is mentioned in a great many folk songs. The men also enjoy ''quaffing'' (drinking) a draught (draft—a drink) now and then from the ''jug,'' probably full of corn whiskey.

Verse eight is given over to a description of nature. They sleep in a ''brake and bog'' (swampy ground overgrown with bushes); an owl hoots; a ''cooter'' (turtle) crawls by; and an alligator splashes into the pond.

In verse nine, they ride out in a moonless night to attack (verse ten) the ''Tory camp'' (British).

Francis Marion, ''The Swamp Fox,'' was a small, thin, and sickly-looking man, but he will always be remembered for his heroic deeds in the bitter struggle for American independence in the Carolinas.

THE SWAMP FOX

1. We__ fol - low where__ the Swamp__ Fox guides, His friends__ and mer - ry men__ are we; And__ when__ the troop__ of Tarle - ton rides, We bur - row in__ the cy - press tree. The turf - y tus - sock is__ our bed, Our home is in__ the red__ deer's den, Our__ roof__ the tree__ top o - ver - head, For__ we__ are wild__ and hunt - ed men.

2.
We fly by day, and shun its light;
But, prompt to strike the sudden blow,
We mount, and start with early night,
And through the forest track our foe.
And soon he hears our chargers leap,
The flashing saber blinds his eyes,
And ere he drives away his sleep,
And rushes from his camp, he dies.

3.
Free bridle-bit, good gallant steed,
That will not ask a kind caress,
To swim the Santee at our need,
When on his heels the foemen press—
The true heart and the ready hand,
The spirit stubborn to be free—
The twisted bore, the smiting brand—
And we are Marion's men you see.

4.
Now light the fire, and cook the meal,
The last, perhaps, that we shall taste;
I hear the Swamp-Fox round us steal, .
And that's a sign we move in haste.
He whistles to the scouts, and, hark!
You hear his order calm and low—
Come, wave your torch across the dark,
And let us see the boys that go.

5.
We may not see their forms again,
God help 'em should they find the strife,
For they are strong and fearless men,
And make no coward terms for life:
They'll fight as long as Marion bids,
And when he speaks the word to shy,
Then—not till then—they turn their steeds,
Through thickening shade and swamp to fly.

6.
Now stir the fire, and lie at ease;
The scouts are gone, and on the brush
I see the colonel bend his knees,
To take his slumbers, too—but, hush!
He's praying, comrades: 'tis not strange;
The man that's fighting day by day,
May well, when night comes, take a change,
And down upon his knees to pray.

7.
Break up that hoecake, boys, and hand
The sly and silent jug that's there;
I love not it should idle stand
When Marion's men have need of cheer.
'Tis seldom that our luck affords
A stuff like this we just have quaff'd,
And dry potatoes on our boards
May always call for such a draught.

8.
Now pile the brush and roll the log:
Hard pillow, but a soldier's head,
That's half the time in brake and bog,
Must never think of softer bed.
The owl is hooting to the night,
The cooter crawling o'er the bank,
And in that pond the plashing light
Tells where the alligator sank.

9.
What—'tis the signal! start so soon?
And through the Santee swamp so deep,
Without the aid of friendly moon,
And we, heaven help us, half asleep!
But courage, comrades, Marion leads,
The Swamp-Fox takes us out tonight;
So clear your swords, and coax your steeds,
There's goodly chance, I think, of fight.

10.
We follow where the Swamp-Fox guides,
We leave the swamp and cypress tree,
Our spurs are in our coursers' sides,
And ready for the strife are we.
The Tory camp is now in sight,
And there he cowers within his den;
He hears our shout, he dreads the fight,
He fears, and flies from Marion's men.

General Washington stands with French general Rochambeau, who is inspecting the trenches at Yorktown. British general Cornwallis's surrender here in 1781 was the last battle of the war.

The Surrender of Cornwallis

In 1778, France joined America in the war against England. By 1780, French naval and military assistance was playing an important role in the ongoing struggle for independence.

So it was that when British general Charles Cornwallis and American general Nathanael Greene were battling each other across the Carolinas during 1780 and 1781, the British were constantly looking over their shoulders to see if the French navy was anywhere in sight.

By September 1781, Cornwallis found himself in Yorktown, Virginia, on Chesapeake Bay. He had his back to the water, and Washington, now in personal command of the patriot campaign, had him trapped. Cornwallis's worst fears were realized when French admiral François De Grasse sailed into the bay with a fleet of twenty-four ships to support Washington's troops.

A smaller British fleet of nineteen ships that had been anchored in the bay realized that they could not stand up to the French. They set sail for New York, leaving Cornwallis to fight the patriot troops alone. By September 28, Washington and his French allies had completely sealed off the British army.

British general Sir Henry Clinton, who was stationed in New York, sent a message to Cornwallis, stating that a British fleet of twenty-six ships and five thousand troops would sail to his rescue on October 5. Time was running out for Cornwallis. By October 13, his reinforcements had still not shown up.

The British tried to break out of the trap by retreating across the York River and heading south. Washington's troops held firm. Cornwallis finally realized that Clinton's troops would never reach him in time. His supplies were nearly all gone. There was only one choice: surrender.

On October 17, the terms of surrender were agreed upon, and the formal laying down of arms took place on October 19, 1781. It took three days for the news to reach Philadelphia, where the United States Congress was in session.

''The Surrender of Cornwallis'' begins with the words, ''Come all you bold Americans. . . .'' This opening line follows the traditional form

American statesman Benjamin Franklin discusses the Treaty of Paris with
Richard Oswald, a representative of the British government. Two years passed
after Cornwallis surrendered at Yorktown before the peace treaty was approved.

of a narrative ballad, where the singer urges his listeners to pay attention to what he has to say. The phrase, ''Come all you . . .'' was so commonly used that this type of song was called a ''come all you,'' or ''come all ye'' ballad.

In verse two, Lord Cornwallis is politely insulted by comparing him to ''poor Burgoyne,'' who surrendered to the Americans at Saratoga four years earlier.

''Blackamores,'' in verse five, were black men who fought on the British side. In verse six, ''Sir Harry'' refers to Sir Henry Clinton.

In verse seven, ''Greene'' is General Nathanael Greene, who, under Washington, commanded American troops in the Carolinas. He was a comrade-in-arms of ''The Swamp Fox.''

> *The Battle of Yorktown was the last important operation of the war. King George III realized that the war was lost. American independence was recognized as a fact. After much discussion and negotiation, a formal peace treaty between Great Britain and the new United States of America was signed in Paris on September 3, 1783.*

THE SURRENDER OF CORNWALLIS

2.

A summons to surrender
Was sent unto the Lord,
Which made him feel like poor Burgoyne
And quickly draw his sword,
"Must I give o'er these glittering troops,
These ships and Hessians, too,
And yield to General Washington
And his bold rebel crew?"

3.

A council to surrender,
This lord did then command,
"What say you, my brave heroes,
To yield you must depend;
For don't you see the bomb-shells fly,
And cannons loud do roar,
DeGrasse is in the harbor
And Washington's on shore."

4.

'Twas the nineteenth of October
In the year of eighty-one,
Cornwallis did surrender
To General Washington.
Six thousand chosen British troops
Marched out and grounded arms,
Huzza, ye bold Americans,
For now sweet music charms.

5.

Six thousand chosen British troops
To Washington resigned,
Besides some ships and Hessians,
That could not stay behind;
With refugees and blackamores,
Oh, what a direful crew!
It was then he had some thousands,
But now he's got but few.

6.

My Lord has gone unto new York,
Sir Harry for to see;
For to send home this dreadful news
Unto his Majesty:
To contradict some former lines
Which he before had sent,
That he and his bold British troops
Would conquer where they went.

7.

Here's a health to General Washington,
And his brave army, too,
And likewise to our worthy Greene,
To him much honor's due.
May we subdue those English troops
And clear the eastern shore,
That we may live in peace, my boys,
Whilst wars they are no more.

After the surrender of Cornwallis, people began thinking of the war as *history*. "The spirit of '76," meaning the patriotic spirit surrounding the signing of the Declaration of Independence on July 4, 1776, was a common expression. Anything having to do with the war could be referred to as "the spirit of '76," even if it had taken place some other year.

"In the Days of Seventy-Six" is a happy song that boils down the war into four battles. It is sung to the tune of the English folk song "The Lincolnshire Poacher," a rollicking song about the delights of poaching (hunting illegally) on royal land in "merry olde England." The jubilant mood of the first battle of the war at Lexington is set by using some of the chorus from "The Lincolnshire Poacher": "O, 'tis my delight on a starry night, in the season of the year."

In verse two we find ourselves in Pennsylvania, on the banks of the Delaware River across from Trenton, New Jersey. All through November 1776, the American army had been driven out of New York, across New Jersey and across the Delaware into Pennsylvania. George Washington's ragged army had been reduced to a smaller and smaller force as many discouraged soldiers simply deserted and went home. As winter set in and snow began to fall, life became increasingly hard for the few remaining patriot soldiers.

Across the river from Washington's camp, the British settled in for the winter at Trenton. It was just too cold to fight—or so they thought.

On Christmas night, 1776, General Washington put a daring plan into action. Knowing that the enemy would be tired and off guard after celebrating Christmas, he and his men quietly rowed across the icy Delaware under cover of darkness, in hopes of reaching the other shore by dawn.

The plan was successful. The surprised sleeping enemy soldiers were completely routed. Of the more than 1,200 Hessian mercenaries, 106 were killed and 950 captured. The American losses were five or six wounded. As the song aptly says: "They gave the foe a drubbing."

Verse three finds us at the battles of Saratoga and Yorktown, while verse four sends a warning to any who would be foolish enough to attack "Columbia's sons," a poetic expression for Americans.

One of the most daring acts of the Revolutionary War was Washington's crossing
of the Delaware River to surprise sleeping Hessian troops on Christmas night.

IN THE DAYS OF SEVENTY–SIX

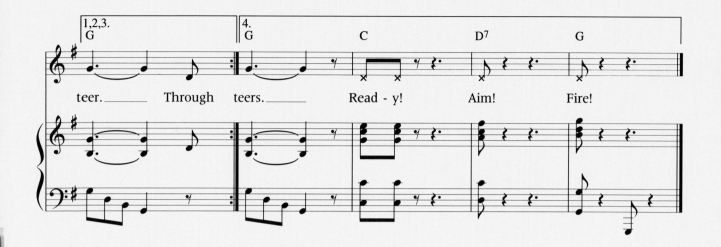

teer._____ Through   teers._____   Read - y!   Aim!   Fire!

2.
Through snow and ice at Trenton, boys,
They crossed the Delaware,
Led on by immortal Washington
No danger did they fear.
They gave the foe a drubbing, boys,
Then back to town did steer. *Chorus*

3.
At Saratoga next, my boys,
Burgoyne they beat severe;
And at the siege of Yorktown
They gained their cause so dear;
Cornwallis there gave up his sword,
Whilst Freedom's sons did cheer. *Chorus*

4.
And should a foeman e'er again
Upon our coast appear,
There's hearts around me, brave and true,
Who'd quickly volunteer
To drive invaders from the soil
Columbia's sons hold dear.

FINAL CHORUS:
O, they'd each delight to march and fight
Like Yankee volunteers.
Spoken: READY! AIM! FIRE!

The colonies declared their independence from Great Britain on July 4, 1776. It took seven years full of bloodshed and killing before peace was declared and Americans were truly set free.

A Final Note

The war was over. The British sailed back to England, and the American soldiers and their families got down to the real business of making the new country work. The songs they had sung still echoed over the land. The broadsides, which had served as colonial and revolutionary newspapers, became part of the history of the brand-new United States of America.

People now sang the songs with a feeling of nostalgia, thinking of the "days of '76" and retelling the old stories of heroic men and their famous deeds.

As our country moved into the nineteenth century, other wars, other battles, and other heroes were sung about as well. The musical language of these newer songs took on a different feeling—less English sounding, more American in melody and rhythm. The style of the words changed also. Language, as well as musical style, changes and develops over time.

What remains the same, however, are the basic feelings expressed in soldiers' songs, no matter what period of history they spring from. A young man marching off to war has mixed emotions: pride, fear, hope, and homesickness; the realization that there is a job to be done; and the desire to get it over with and to return home in one piece.

While references to "the spirit of '76" never fail to stir patriotic sentiments in the hearts of Americans, we must always remember that wars—all wars—have losers as well as winners, and that it is the youth of the country that is called upon to make the greatest sacrifices. While we proudly sing the songs from the American Revolution, the songs from the time that witnessed the birth of our nation, we must never forget every victory was paid for by men on both sides of the line.

> Here I sit on Buttermilk Hill,
> Who could blame me, cry my fill?
> And every tear would turn a mill:
> Johnny has gone for a soldier.

FURTHER READING

About Songs

Amazing Grace: The Story Behind the Song by Jim Haskins. Brookfield, Conn.: The Millbrook Press, 1992.

American History Songbook by Jerry Silverman. Pacific, Mo.: Mel Bay Publications, 1992.

From Sea to Shining Sea: A Treasury of American Folklore and Folk Songs compiled by Amy L. Cohn. New York: Scholastic Inc., 1993.

Songs of America by Don Cooper. New York: Random House, 1990.

About the Revolutionary War

Valley Forge by Libby Hughes. New York: Macmillan, 1993.

The American Revolution by Francine Sabin. Mahwah, N.J.: Troll Associates, 1985.

The Revolutionary War: A Sourcebook on Colonial America by Carter Smith. Brookfield, Conn.: The Millbrook Press, 1991.

INDEX

ABOUT THE AUTHOR

Jerry Silverman is a professional folksinger and guitarist. He has devoted his time and considerable talent to teaching and performing in schools all over the country. Since publishing his first songbook in 1958, he has written more than one hundred books—method books and songbooks organized around international and American themes.

Silverman lives in Hastings-on-Hudson, New York, with his wife and three sons.

DATE			